# Common prayer Collection

## Leunig

He that shuts Love out, in turn shall be
Shut out from Love, and on her threshold lie
Howling in the outer darkness.

TENNYSON

Love is like bread. It has to be made fresh every day.

OLD SAYING

Love is the bright foreigner, the foreign self.

EMERSON

CollinsDove
A Division of HarperCollins*Publishers*

Published by Collins Dove
A Division of HarperCollins*Publishers* (Australia) Pty Ltd
22-24 Joseph Street
North Blackburn, Victoria 3130

First published separately as *A Common Prayer* (1990) and
*The Prayer Tree* (1991)
This combined edition first published 1993
Designed by William Hung
Cover design by William Hung
Cover illustration by Michael Leunig

Typeset in Meridien by EMS Typesetting
Printed by McPherson's Printing Group

The National Library of Australia
Cataloguing-in-Publication Data:

  Leunig, Michael, 1945-
  Common prayer collection

  ISBN 1 86371 231 3.

  1. Prayers. I. Leunig, Michael, 1945-  . Common prayer.
  II. Leunig, Michael, 1945-  . Prayer tree. III. Title. IV. Title:
  Common prayer. V. Title: Prayer tree.

242.8

To

Anne Clancy and Helga Leunig

# Introduction to
## *A Common Prayer*

I have drawn a simple picture of a person kneeling
before a duck to symbolise and demonstrate my
ideas and feelings about the nature of prayer. I ask
the reader to bear with the absurdity of the image
and to remember that the search for the sublime
may sometimes have a ridiculous beginning.
Here then is the story behind the picture.

A man kneels before a duck in a sincere attempt to
talk with it. This is a clear depiction of irrational
behaviour and an important aspect of prayer.
Let us put this aside for the moment and move
on to the particulars.

The act of kneeling in the picture symbolises
humility. The upright stance has been abandoned
because of the human attitudes and qualities it
represents: power, stature, control, rationality,
worldliness, pride and ego. The kneeling man
knows, as everybody does, that a proud and
upright man does not and cannot talk with a duck.
So the upright stance is rejected. The man kneels.
He humbles himself. He comes closer to the duck.

He becomes more like the duck. He does these things because it improves his chances of communicating with it.

The duck in the picture symbolises one thing and many things: nature, instinct, feeling, beauty, innocence, the primal, the non-rational and the mysterious unsayable; qualities we can easily attribute to a duck and qualities which, coincidentally and remarkably, we can easily attribute to the inner life of the kneeling man, to his spirit or his soul. The duck then, in this picture, can be seen as a symbol of the human spirit, and in wanting connection with his spirit it is a symbolic picture of a man searching for his soul.

The person cannot actually see this 'soul' as he sees the duck in the picture but he can feel its enormous impact on his life. Its outward manifestations can be disturbing and dramatic and its inner presence is often wild and rebellious or elusive and difficult to grasp: but the person knows that from this inner dimension, with all its turmoil, comes his love and his fear, his creative spark, his music, his art and his very will to live. He also feels that a strong relationship with this inner world seems to lead to a good relationship with the world around him and a better life. Conversely, he feels

that alienation from these qualities, or loss of
spirit, seems to cause great misery and loneliness.

He believes in this spiritual dimension, this inner
life, and he knows that it can be strengthened by
acknowledgement and by giving it a name.

He may call it the human spirit, he may call it the
soul or he may call it god. The particular name is
not so very important.

The point is that he acknowledges this spiritual
dimension. He would be a fool to ignore it, so
powerful is its effect on his life, so joyous,
so mysterious, so frightening.

Not only does he recognise and name it but he is
intensely curious about it. He wants to explore it
and familiarise himself with its ways and its depth.
He wants a robust relationship with it, he wants
to trust it, he wants its advice and the vitality it
provides. He also wants to feed it, this inner world,
to care for it and make it strong. It's important
to him.

And the more he does these things, this coming
to terms with his soul, the more his life takes on
a sense of meaning. The search for the spirit leads

to love and a better world, for him and for those around him. This personal act is also a social and political act because it affects so many people who may be connected to the searcher.

But how do we search for our soul, our god, our inner voice? How do we find this treasure hidden in our life? How do we connect to this transforming and healing power? It seems as difficult as talking to a bird. How indeed?

There are many ways, all of them involving great struggle, and each person must find his or her own way. The search and the relationship is a lifetime's work and there is much help available, but an important, perhaps essential part of this process seems to involve an ongoing, humble acknowledgement of the soul's existence and integrity. Not just an intellectual recognition but also a ritualistic, perhaps poetic, gesture of acknowledgement: a respectful tribute.

Why it should need to be like this is mysterious, but a ceremonial affirmation, no matter how small, seems to carry an indelible and resonant quality into the heart which the intellect is incapable of carrying.

Shaking the hand of a friend is such a ritual.
It reaffirms something deep and unsayable in the
relationship. A non-rational ritual acknowledges
and reaffirms a non-rational, but important, part
of the relationship. It is a small but vital thing.

This ritual of recognition and connection is
repeatable and each time it occurs something
important is revitalised and strengthened.
The garden is watered.

And so it is with the little ritual which recognises
the inner life and attempts to connect to it.
This do-it-yourself ceremony where the mind is on
its knees; the small ceremony of words which calls
on the soul to come forth. This ritual known
simply as prayer.

The garden is watered.

A person kneels before a duck and speaks to it
with sincerity. The person is praying.

Christmas.

Dear God, it is timely that we give thanks for the lives of all prophets, teachers, healers and revolutionaries, living and dead, acclaimed or obscure, who have rebelled, worked and suffered for the cause of love and joy.

We also celebrate that part of us, that part within ourselves, which has rebelled, worked and suffered for the cause of love and joy.

We give thanks and celebrate.
Amen.

God help us to change. To change ourselves
and to change our world. To know the need
for it. To deal with the pain of it. To feel the
joy of it. To undertake the journey without
understanding the destination. The art of
gentle revolution.

Amen.

God give us strength. Strength to hold on
and strength to let go.
Amen.

That which is Christ-like within us shall be crucified. It shall suffer and be broken. And that which is Christ-like within us shall rise up. It shall love and create.

Dear God,

We give thanks for the darkness of the
night where lies the world of dreams. Guide
us closer to our dreams so that we may be
nourished by them. Give us good dreams
and memory of them so that we may carry
their poetry and mystery into our daily lives.

Grant us deep and restful sleep that we
may wake refreshed with strength enough to
renew a world grown tired.

We give thanks for the inspiration of stars,
the dignity of the moon and the lullabies of
crickets and frogs.

Let us restore the night and reclaim it as
a sanctuary of peace, where silence shall be
music to our hearts and darkness shall
throw light upon our souls. Good night.
Sweet dreams.
Amen.

God give us rain when we expect sun.
Give us music when we expect trouble.
Give us tears when we expect breakfast.
Give us dreams when we expect a storm.
Give us a stray dog when we expect
   congratulations.
God play with us, turn us sideways and
   around.
Amen.

Dear God,

We give thanks for birds. All types of birds. Small birds and large birds. Domestic fowls, migratory birds and birds of prey, hooting birds, whistling birds, shrikes, colored parrots and dark darting wrens. Birds too numerous to mention. We praise them all.

We mourn the loss of certain species and pray for the deliverance of endangered ones. We pray, too, for farm birds, that they may be released from cruelty and suffering.

We give thanks for eggs and feathers, for brave, cheerful songs in the morning and the wonderful, haunting, night prayers of owls, mopokes, frogmouths and all nocturnal fowls.

We praise the character of birds, their constancy, their desire for freedom, their flair for music and talent for flying. May we always marvel at their ability to fly. Especially we praise their disregard for the human hierarchy and the ease with which they leave their droppings on the heads of commoners

or kings regardless. Grant them fair weather,
fresh food and abundant materials for
building their nests in spring. Provide them
too with perches and roosts with pleasant
aspects. Dear God, guide our thoughts to the
joy and beauty of birds. Feathered angels.
May they always be above us.
Amen.

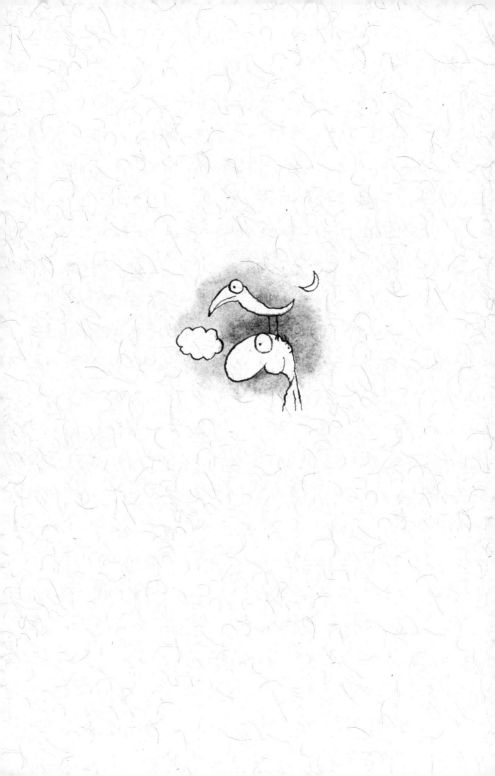

Dear God,

Give comfort and peace to those who are separated from loved ones. May the ache in their hearts be the strengthening of their hearts. May their longing bring resolve to their lives, conviction and purity to their love. Teach them to embrace their sadness lest it turn to despair. Transform their yearning into wisdom. Let their hearts grow fonder.

Amen.

There are only two feelings. Love and fear.
There are only two languages. Love and fear.
There are only two activities. Love and fear.
There are only two motives, two procedures,
two frameworks, two results. Love and fear.
Love and fear.

Dear God,
These circumstances will change. This
situation shall pass.
Amen.

God bless the lost, the confused, the unsure,
the bewildered, the puzzled, the mystified,
the baffled, and the perplexed.
Amen.

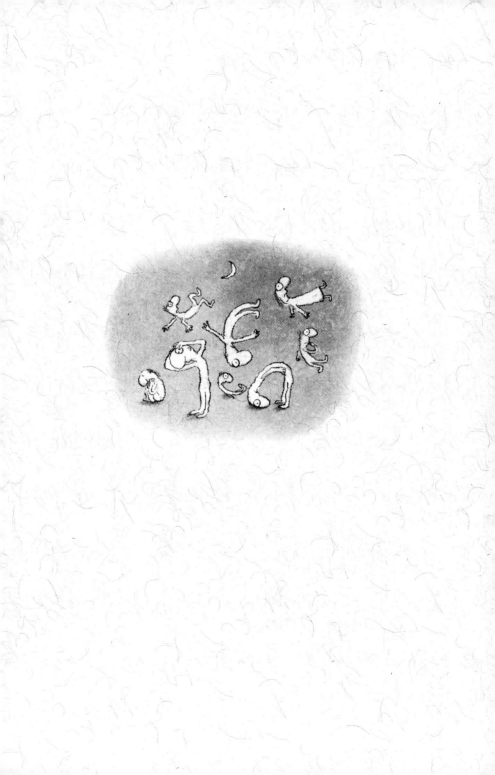

It is time to plant tomatoes. Dear God, we praise this fruit and give thanks for its life and evolution. We salute the tomato, cheery, fragrant morsel, beloved provider, survivor and thriver and giver of life. Giving and giving and giving. Plump with summer's joy. The scent of its stem is summer's joy, is promise and rapture. Its branches breathe perfume of promise and rapture. Giving and giving and giving.

Dear God, give strength to the wings and knees of pollinating bees, give protection from hailstorms, gales and frosts, give warm days and quenching rains. Refresh and adorn our gardens and our tables. Refresh us with tomatoes.

Rejoice and rejoice! Celebrate the scarlet soul of winter sauces. Behold the delicious flavor! Behold the oiled vermilion moons that ride and dive in olive-bobbing seas of vinegared lettuce. Let us rejoice! Let this rejoicing be our thanks for tomatoes. Amen.

Dear God,

Let us prepare for winter. The sun
has turned away from us and the nest of
summer hangs broken in a tree. Life slips
through our fingers and, as darkness gathers,
our hands grow cold. It is time to go inside.
It is time for reflection and resonance. It is
time for contemplation. Let us go inside.
Amen.

Let us pray for wisdom. Let us pause from thinking and empty our mind. Let us stop the noise. In the silence let us listen to our heart. The heart which is buried alive. Let us be still and wait and listen carefully. A sound from the deep, from below. A faint cry. A weak tapping. Distant muffled feelings from within. The cry for help.

We shall rescue the entombed heart. We shall bring it to the surface, to the light and the air. We shall nurse it and listen respectfully to its story. The heart's story of pain and suffocation, of darkness and yearning. We shall help our feelings to live in the sun. Together again we shall find relief and joy.

Dear God,

We struggle, we grow weary, we grow tired.
We are exhausted, we are distressed, we
despair. We give up, we fall down, we let go.
We cry. We are empty, we grow calm, we are
ready. We wait quietly.

A small, shy truth arrives. Arrives from
without and within. Arrives and is born.
Simple, steady, clear. Like a mirror, like a
bell, like a flame. Like rain in summer. A
precious truth arrives and is born within us.
Within our emptiness.

We accept it, we observe it, we absorb it.
We surrender to our bare truth. We are
nourished, we are changed. We are blessed.
We rise up.

For this we give thanks.
Amen.

Dear God,

We pray for balance and exchange.
Balance us like trees. As the roots of a tree
shall equal its branches so must the inner
life be equal to the outer life. And as the
leaves shall nourish the roots so shall the
roots give nourishment to the leaves.
Without equality and exchange of
nourishment there can be no growth
and no love.
Amen.

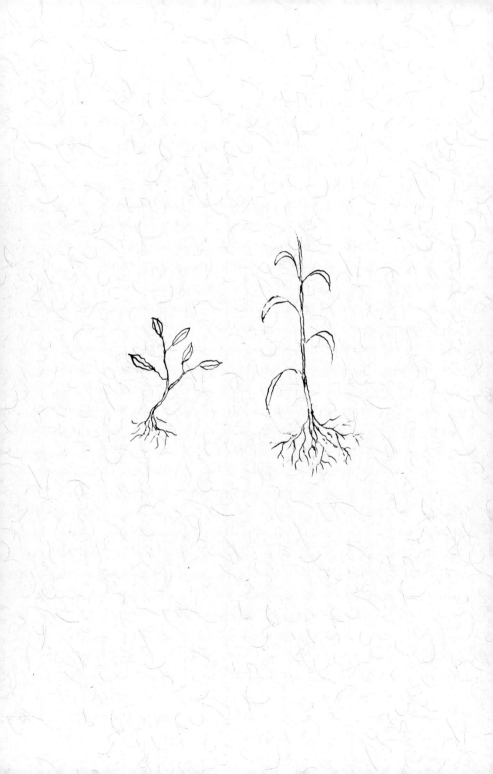

Dear God,

We give thanks for places of simplicity
and peace. Let us find such a place within
ourselves. We give thanks for places of refuge
and beauty. Let us find such a place within
ourselves. We give thanks for places of
nature's truth and freedom, of joy,
inspiration and renewal, places where
all creatures may find acceptance and
belonging. Let us search for these places: in
the world, in ourselves and in others. Let us
restore them. Let us strengthen and protect
them and let us create them.

May we mend this outer world according
to the truth of our inner life and may our
soul be shaped and nourished by nature's
eternal wisdom.
Amen.

God be with the mother. As she carried
her child may she carry her soul. As her
child was born, may she give birth and life
and form to her own, higher truth. As she
nourished and protected her child, may she
nourish and protect her inner life and her
independence. For her soul shall be her
most painful birth, her most difficult child
and the dearest sister to her other children.
Amen.

God help us. With great skill and energy we have ignored the state of the human heart. With politics and economics we have denied the heart's needs. With eloquence, wit and reason we have belittled the heart's wisdom. With sophistication and style, with science and technology, we have drowned out the voice of the soul. The primitive voice, the innocent voice. The truth. We cannot hear our heart's truth and thus we have betrayed and belittled ourselves and pledged madness to our children. With skill and pride we have made for ourselves an unhappy society. God be with us.
Amen.

God be amongst us and within us. Earth is
our mother and nature's law is our father,
our protector. Thus, we pray.

Father do not forgive them for they know
precisely what they do. Those destroyers of
earth's beauty and goodness, those killers
of nature, do not forgive them.

Those betrayers of nature's love.
Those exploiters of nature's innocence.
Those poisoners. Do not forgive them.

Those greedy, pompous people. That
greed and pomposity within us all. The sum
total of that petty greed and pomposity
within us all. We now know precisely what
these things are doing to this earth. So
Father, do not forgive us for we now
understand what it is that we do.
Amen.

We pray for the fragile ecology of the
heart and the mind. The sense of meaning.
So finely assembled and balanced and so
easily overturned. The careful, ongoing
construction of love. As painful and
exhausting as the struggle for truth
and as easily abandoned.

Hard fought and won are the shifting
sands of this sacred ground, this ecology.
Easy to desecrate and difficult to defend,
this vulnerable joy, this exposed faith,
this precious order. This sanity.

We shall be careful. With others and
with ourselves.
Amen.

Dear God,

We celebrate spring's returning and the rejuvenation of the natural world. Let us be moved by this vast and gentle insistence that goodness shall return, that warmth and life shall succeed, and help us to understand our place within this miracle. Let us see that as a bird now builds its nest, bravely, with bits and pieces, so we must build human faith. It is our simple duty; it is the highest art; it is our natural and vital role within the miracle of spring: the creation of faith.

Amen.

God accept our prayers.

Send us tears in return.

Give freedom to this exchange.

Let us pray inwardly.

Let us weep outwardly.

This is the breathing of the soul.

This is the vitality of the spirit.

For this we give thanks.

Amen.

Dear God,

When we fall, let us fall inwards. Let us fall freely and completely: that we may find our depth and humility: the solid earth from which we may rise up and love again.
Amen.

Dear God,
We loosen our grip.
We open our hand.
We are accepting.
In our empty hand
We feel the shape
Of simple eternity.
It nestles there.
We hold it gently.
We are accepting.
Amen.

We give thanks for domestic animals.
Those creatures who can trust us enough to
come close. Those creatures who can trust us
enough to be true to themselves.

They approach us from the wild. They
approach us from the inner world. They
bring beauty and joy, comfort and peace.

For this miracle and for the lesson of this
miracle. We give thanks.
Amen.

The path to your door
It the path within:
Is made by animals,
Is lined by flowers,
Is lined by thorns,
Is stained with wine,
Is lit by the lamp of sorrowful dreams:
Is washed with joy,
Is swept by grief,
Is blessed by the lonely traffic of art:
Is known by heart,
Is known by prayer,
Is lost and found,
Is always strange,
The path to your door.

'Love one another and you will be happy.'
It's as simple and as difficult as that. There is
no other way.
Amen.

# Introduction to
## *The Prayer Tree*

A person kneels to contemplate a tree and to
reflect upon the troubles and joys of life.

It is difficult to accept that life is difficult; that love
is not easy and that doubt and struggle, suffering
and failure, are inevitable for each and every one
of us.

We seek life's ease. We yearn for joy and release,
for flowers and the sun. And although we may
find these in abundance we also find ourselves
lying awake at night possessed by the terrible fear
that life is impossible. Sometimes when we least
expect it we wake up overwhelmed by a massive
sense of loneliness, misery, chaos and death:
appalled by the agony and futility of existence.

It is difficult indeed to accept that this darkness
belongs naturally and importantly to our human
condition and that we must live with it and bear it.
It seems so unbearable.

Nature, however, requires that we have the darkness of our painful feelings and that we respect it and make a bold place for it in our lives. Without its recognition and acceptance there can be no true sense of life's great depth, wherein lies our capacity to love, to create and to make meaning.

Nature requires that we form a relationship between our joy and our despair, that they not remain divided or hidden from one another. For these are the feelings which must cross-polinate and inform each other in order that the soul be enlivened and strong. It is the soul, after all, which bears the burden of our experience. It is the soul through which we love and it is the soul which senses most faithfully our function within the integrity of the natural world.

Nature requires that we be soulful and therefore requires a dimension within us where darkness and light may meet and know each other. Mornings and evenings somewhere inside, with similar qualities to the mornings and the evenings of the earth. Qualities of gradual but vast change; of stillness and tender transference, fading and emerging, foreboding and revelation.

Mornings and evenings: the traditional times for
prayer and the singing of birds, times of graceful
light whereby the heart may envisage its poetry
and describe for us what it sees.

But how do we find the mornings and evenings
within? How do we establish and behold them and
be affected by their gentle atmospheres and small
miracles? How do we enter this healing twilight?

The matter requires our imagination. In particular,
it requires the aspect of imagination we have
comes to know as prayer.

We pray. We imagine our way inwards and
downwards and there, with heartfelt thoughts or
words we declare our fears and our yearnings;
we call out for love and forgiveness; we proclaim
our responsibility and gratitude. The struggling,
grounded soul speaks to the higher spirit and thus
we exist in the mornings and the evenings of the
heart: thus we are affected and changed by the
qualities we have created within ourselves.

Might not prayer then be our most accessible
means to inner reconciliation; a natural healing
function in response to the pain of the divided self

and the divided world? Might not prayerfulness be part of our survival instinct belonging more to the wilderness than to the church?

And just as we have become somewhat alienated from nature and its cycles, could it be that we are also estranged from our instinctive capacity for prayer and need to understand it afresh from the example of the natural world?

The person contemplates the tree.

The tree sends it roots beneath the surface, seeking nourishment in the dark soil: the rich "broken down" matter of life.

As they reach down and search, the roots hold the tree firmly to the earth.

Thus held and nourished, the tree grows upwards into the light, drinking the sun and air and expressing its truth: its branches and foliage, its flowers and fruit. Life swarms around and into it. Birds and insects teem within its embrace, carrying pollen and seed. They nest and breed and sing and buzz. They glorify the creation.

The tree changes as its grows. It is torn by wind and lightning, scarred by frost and fire. Branches die and new ones emerge. The drama of existence has its way with the tree but still it grows; still its roots reach down into the darkness; still its branches flow with sap and reach upward and outward into the world.

A person kneels to contemplate a tree and to reflect upon the troubles and joys of life.
The person imagines mornings and evenings in a great forest of prayers, swarming and teeming with life.

The person is learning how to pray.

Love is born
With a dark and troubled face
When hope is dead
And in the most unlikely place
Love is born:
Love is always born.

God let us be serious.
Face to face.
Heart to heart.
Let us be fully present.
Strongly present.
Deeply serious.
The closest we may come
to innocence.
Amen

We welcome summer and the glorious
blessing of light. We are rich with light;
we are loved by the sun. Let us empty our
hearts into the brilliance. Let us pour our
darkness into the glorious, forgiving light.
For this loving abundance let us give thanks
and offer our joy.
Amen

We give thanks for the life and work of
Wolfgang Amadeus Mozart. Let us celebrate
and praise all those musicians and
composers who give their hands and hearts
and voices to the expression of life's mystery
and joy.
Who nourish our heart in its yearning.
Who dignify our soul in its struggling.
Who harmonise our grief and gladness.
Who make melody from the fragments
    of chaos.
Who align our spirit with creation.
Who reveal to us the grace of God.
Who calm us and delight us and set us free
    to love and forgive.
Let us give thanks and rejoice.
Amen

God bless our contradictions, those parts of
us which seem out of character. Let us be
boldly and gladly out of character. Let us be
creatures of paradox and variety: creatures
of contrast; of light and shade: creatures of
faith. God be our constant. Let us step out
of character into the unknown, to struggle
and love and do what we will.
Amen

God help us with ideas, those thoughts
which inform the way we live and the things
we do. Let us not seize upon ideas, neither
shall we hunt them down nor steal them
away. Rather let us wait faithfully for
them to approach, slowly and gently like
creatures from the wild. And let them
enter willingly into our hearts and come
and go freely within the sanctuary of our
contemplation, informing our souls as
they arrive and being enlivened by the
inspiration of our hearts as they leave.

These shall be our truest thoughts. Our
willing and effective ideas. Let us treasure
their humble originality. Let us follow them
gently back into the world with faith that
they shall lead us to lives of harmony and
integrity.
Amen

God help us to find our confession;
The truth within us which is hidden from
   our mind;
The beauty or the ugliness we see elsewhere
But never in ourselves;
The stowaway which has been smuggled
Into the dark side of the heart,
Which puts the heart off balance and causes
   it pain,

Which wearies and confuses us,
Which tips us in false directions and inclines
    us to destruction,
The load which is not carried squarely
Because it is carried in ignorance.
God help us to find our confession.
Help us across the boundary of our
    understanding.

Lead us into the darkness that we may find
    what lies concealed;
That we may confess it towards the light;
That we may carry our truth in the centre
    of our heart;
That we may carry our cross wisely
And bring harmony into our life and
    our world.
Amen

God rest us.

Rest that part of us which is tired.

Awaken that part of us which is asleep.

God awaken us and awake within us.

Amen

We give thanks for the mystery of hair.
Too little here and too much there.
Censored and shaved, controlled and
    suppressed:
Unwelcome guest in soups and sandwiches.
Difficult growth always needing attention.
Gentle and comforting;
Complex and wild;
Reminding us softly
That we might be animals.
Growing and growing
'Til the day that we die.

And the day after as well
So they say!
In all of its places
And in all of its ways
We give thanks for the blessing of hair.
Amen

God be with those who explore in the cause
of understanding; whose search takes them
far from what is familiar and comfortable
and leads them into danger or terrifying
loneliness. Let us try to understand their
sometimes strange or difficult ways; their
confronting or unusual language; the
uncommon life of their emotions, for they
have been affected and shaped and changed
by their struggle at the frontiers of a wild
darkness, just as we may be affected,
shaped and changed by the insights they
bring back to us. Bless them with strength
and peace.
Amen

God help us to live slowly:
To move simply:
To look softly:
To allow emptiness:
To let the heart create for us.
Amen

In order to be truthful
We must do more than speak the truth.
We must also hear truth.
We must also receive truth.
We must also act upon truth.
We must also search for truth.
The difficult truth.
Within us and around us.
We must devote ourselves to truth.
Otherwise we are dishonest
And our lives are mistaken.
God grant us the strength and the courage
To be truthful.
Amen

Dear God, we pray for another way of
being: another way of knowing.

Across the difficult terrain of our existence
we have attempted to build a highway and
in so doing have lost our footpath. God lead
us to our footpath: Lead us there where
in simplicity we may move at the speed of
natural creatures and feel the earth's love
beneath our feet. Lead us there where
step-by-step we may feel the movement of
creation in our hearts. And lead us there
where side-by-side we may feel the embrace
of the common soul. Nothing can be loved at
speed. God lead us to the slow path; to the
joyous insights of the pilgrim; another way
of knowing: another way of being.
Amen

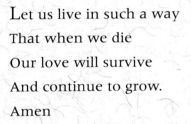

Let us live in such a way
That when we die
Our love will survive
And continue to grow.
Amen

God help us
To rise up from our struggle.
Like a tree rises up from the soil.
Our roots reaching down to our trouble,
Our rich, dark dirt of existence.
Finding nourishment deeply
And holding us firmly.
Always connected.
Growing upwards and into the sun.
Amen

Dear God,
We rejoice and give thanks for earthworms, bees, ladybirds and broody hens; for humans tending their gardens, talking to animals, cleaning their homes and singing to themselves; for the rising of the sap, the fragrance of growth, the invention of the wheelbarrow and the existence of the teapot, we give thanks. We celebrate and give thanks.
Amen

We give thanks for singers.
All types of singers.
Popular, concert singers and tuneless
   singers in the bath.
Whistlers, hummers and those who sing
   while they work.
Singers of lullabies; singers of nonsense and
   small scraps of melody.
Singers on branches and rooftops.
Morning yodellers and evening warblers.
Singers in seedy nightclubs, singers in the
   street;
Singers in cathedrals, school halls,
   grandstands, back yards, paddocks,
   bedrooms, corridors, stairwells and
   places of echo and resonance.

We give praise to all those who give some
   small voice
To the everyday joy of the soul.
Amen

We give thanks for the invention of the handle. Without it there would be many things we couldn't hold on to. As for the things we can't hold on to anyway, let us gracefully accept their ungraspable nature and celebrate all things elusive, fleeting and intangible. They mystify us and make us receptive to truth and beauty. We celebrate and give thanks.

Amen

God bless the lone tunnellers; those rare
individuals whose joy and passion it is to
dig mysterious tunnels beneath the surface
of the earth; who share the soulful purpose
of moles and worms; who labour gleefully
beneath our feet while we bask in the sun
or gaze at the stars; whose pockets and
cuffs are full of soil; who dig faithfully in

darkness, turning left and turning right, not
knowing why or where, but absorbed and
fulfilled nevertheless. Under houses; under
roads and statues; beneath and amongst the
roots of trees; on elbows and knees;
carefully, steadily pawing at their beloved
earth; sniffing and savouring the rich odour
of the dirt; dreaming and delighting in the

blackness; onwards and onwards, not
knowing day or night; unsung, unadorned,
unassuming, unrestrained. Grimy
fingernailed angels of the underworld:
we praise them and give thanks for their
constant, unseen presence and the vast
labyrinth they have created beneath our
existence. We praise them and give thanks.
Amen

Autumn.

We give thanks for the harvest of the
  heart's work;
Seeds of faith planted with faith;
Love nurtured by love;
Courage strengthened by courage.
We give thanks for the fruits of the
  struggling soul,
The bitter and the sweet;
For that which has grown in adversity
And for that which has flourished in
  warmth and grace;
For the radiance of the spirit in autumn
And for that which must now fade and die.
We are blessed and give thanks.
Amen

We give thanks for the blessing of winter:
Season to cherish the heart.
To make warmth and quiet for the heart.
To make soups and broths for the heart.
To cook for the heart and read for the
    heart.
To curl up softly and nestle with the heart.
To sleep deeply and gently at one with
    the heart.
To dream with the heart.
To spend time with the heart.
A long, long time of peace with the heart.
We give thanks for the blessing of winter:
Season to cherish the heart.
Amen

God help us
If our world should grow dark;
And there is no way of seeing or knowing.
Grant us courage and trust
To touch and be touched
To find our way onwards
By feeling.
Amen

God bless those who suffer from the
    common cold.
Nature has entered into them;
Has led them aside and gently lain them low
To contemplate life from the wayside;
To consider human frailty;
To receive the deep and dreamy messages
    of fever.
We give thanks for the insights of this
    humble perspective.
We give thanks for blessings in disguise.
Amen

We simplify our lives.
We live gladly with less.
We let go the illusion that we can possess.
We create instead.
We let go the illusion of mobility.
We travel in stillness. We travel at home.
By candlelight and in stillness,
In the presence of flowers,
We make our pilgrimage.
We simplify our lives.

We give thanks for our friends.

Our dear friends.

We anger each other.

We fail each other.

We share this sad earth, this tender life,

   this precious time.

Such richness. Such wildness.

Together we are blown about.

Together we are dragged along.

All this delight.

All this suffering.

All this forgiving life.

We hold it together.

Amen

God bless this tiny little boat
And me who travels in it.
It stays afloat for years and years
And sinks within a minute.

And so the soul in which we sail,
Unknown by years of thinking,
Is deeply felt and understood
The minute that it's sinking.

We search and we search and yet find no
  meaning.
The search for a meaning leads to despair.
And when we are broken the heart finds its
  moment
To fly and to feel and to work as it will
Through the darkness and mystery and wild
  contradiction.

For this is its freedom, its need and its
    calling;
This is its magic, its strength and its
    knowing.
To heal and make meaning while we walk or
    lie dreaming;
To give birth to love within our surrender;
To mother our faith, our spirit and
    yearning;

While we stumble in darkness the heart
    makes our meaning
And offers it into our life and creation
That we may give meaning to life and
    creation
For we only give meaning we do not
    find meaning:
The thing we can't find is the thing we
    shall give.
To make love complete and to honour
    creation.

When the heart
Is cut or cracked or broken
Do not clutch it
Let the wound lie open

Let the wind
From the good old sea blow in
To bathe the wound with salt
And let it sting.

Let a stray dog lick it
Let a bird lean in the hole and sing
A simple song like a tiny bell
And let it ring